A journey of 150 million kilometres

A journey of eight minutes and 20 seconds

A journey that brings life to a planet

The source of all sunbeams is the

Sun

Beware! Look out for solar winds and giant flares...

FOLLOW THE **HIGHWAY** ┈┈┈┈┈┈┈┈┈┈┈┈┈┈→

This is where our journey starts – 150 million kilometres from Earth.

The Sun is a star. Let's examine this star in more detail.

Select
YOUR BYWAY

The Sun

1 What's it made of?
(AND WHAT'S IN THE MIDDLE OF IT?)

┈┈┈┈→ **BYWAY** TO SHOW ZON

2 How big is it?

┈┈┈→ **BYWAY** TO SHOW ZON

3 How old is it?
(AND HOW WAS IT BORN?)

┈┈┈┈→ **BYWAY** TO SHOW ZON

4 How hot does it get?
(AND WHY DOES IT SHINE?)

┈┈┈┈→ **BYWAY** TO SHOW ZON

5 How does the Sun fit in with the rest of the Universe?
(AND WILL THE SUN LAST FOREVER?)

┈┈┈┈→ **BYWAY** TO SHOW ZON

6 Does the Sun move?
(AND WHAT IS AN ECLIPSE?)

┈┈┈┈→ **BYWAY** TO SHOW ZON

The visible surface of the Sun is called the **PHOTOSPHERE** and has a temperature of 5,500°C. It contains small patches of gas called **GRANULES** that fade away after 5 to 10 minutes. These patches are then replaced by new ones.

Invisible Journeys

Sun

Caroline Grimshaw

TEXT EDITOR IQBAL HUSSAIN

SCIENCE CONSULTANT JOHN STRINGER

FALKIRK COUNCIL
LIBRARY SUPPORT
FOR SCHOOLS

WCN

Invisible Journeys
Sun

CREATIVE AND EDITORIAL DIRECTOR
CONCEPT/FORMAT/DESIGN/TEXT
CAROLINE GRIMSHAW

TEXT EDITOR **IQBAL HUSSAIN**
SCIENCE CONSULTANT **JOHN STRINGER**

ILLUSTRATIONS

NICK DUFFY ※ **SPIKE GERRELL**
CAROLINE GRIMSHAW

THANKS TO

TIM SANPHER COMPUTER IMAGERY
LAURA CARTWRIGHT PICTURE RESEARCH
BRONWEN LEWIS EDITORIAL SUPPORT

TITLES IN THIS SERIES → ※ SUN
※ COMMUNICATION

CONCEIVED AND DESIGNED BY CAROLINE GRIMSHAW FOR
TWO-CAN PUBLISHING LTD
346 OLD STREET
LONDON EC1V 9NQ

FIRST PUBLISHED BY TWO-CAN PUBLISHING LTD IN 1997
IN ASSOCIATION WITH FRANKLIN WATTS

HARDBACK ISBN 1-85434-443-9
PAPERBACK ISBN 1-85434-444-7
DEWEY DECIMAL CLASSIFICATION 523.7

HARDBACK 2 4 6 8 10 9 7 5 3 1
PAPERBACK 2 4 6 8 10 9 7 5 3 1

A CATALOGUE RECORD FOR THIS BOOK IS AVAILABLE
FROM THE BRITISH LIBRARY.

PRINTED IN HONG KONG.

Safety Note Never look directly at the Sun – even through sunglasses or anything else – and never, ever with binoculars or a telescope. If you are out in the hot Sun, protect yourself by putting on sun cream and wearing a wide-brimmed hat.

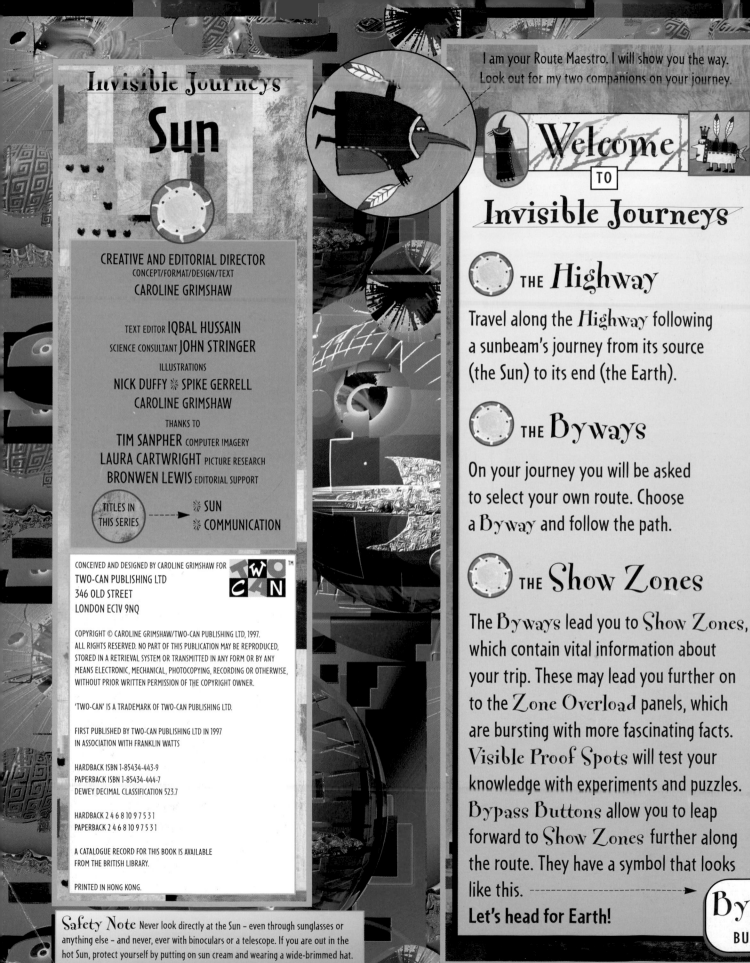

I am your Route Maestro. I will show you the way. Look out for my two companions on your journey.

Welcome
TO
Invisible Journeys

THE Highway

Travel along the *Highway* following a sunbeam's journey from its source (the Sun) to its end (the Earth).

THE Byways

On your journey you will be asked to select your own route. Choose a *Byway* and follow the path.

THE Show Zones

The *Byways* lead you to *Show Zones*, which contain vital information about your trip. These may lead you further on to the *Zone Overload* panels, which are bursting with more fascinating facts. *Visible Proof Spots* will test your knowledge with experiments and puzzles. *Bypass Buttons* allow you to leap forward to *Show Zones* further along the route. They have a symbol that looks like this. ————————→
Let's head for Earth!

Bypass BUTTON

SHOW ZONE

1

What's the Sun made of?

The Sun is a huge glowing ball of hot gases. It is made up almost entirely of two light gases called hydrogen and helium.

How do we know this? Scientists have studied the pattern of coloured lines that make up sunlight. This pattern is called a spectrum. The type of spectrum shows them which chemicals are in the Sun.

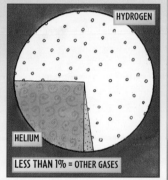

HYDROGEN

HELIUM

LESS THAN 1% = OTHER GASES

AROUND 75% = HYDROGEN This is the lightest and simplest gas known. Hydrogen is vital for various processes that go on in the human body and is also used as a fuel in industry.

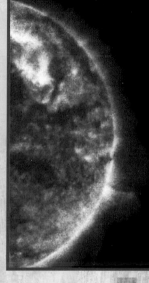

AROUND 25% = HELIUM Scientists discovered this gas on the Sun before they found it on Earth. The name comes from the Greek 'helios' meaning 'sun'. As it is lighter than air, and will not burn like hydrogen, helium is used in scientific balloons. It is also used to help people with breathing difficulties.

LET'S JOURNEY TO THE CENTRE OF THE SUN. FOLLOW THE PATH TO THE **ZONE OVERLOAD**.

◄----- SHOW ZONE 1 ----►

SHOW ZONE

2

How big is the Sun?

The diameter of the Sun is 1,392,000km.

The Sun is in a group of stars astronomers call **YELLOW DWARVES**. Compared with other stars it is only medium-sized. Stars called **SUPERGIANTS** have a diameter 1,000 times that of the Sun.

DOES THE SUN CHANGE SIZE? Only very slightly as it pulsates. In warm countries the Sun may appear bigger because the Earth's atmosphere magnifies our view of the Sun when it is setting.

Visible Proof **SPOT**

Imagine that the Sun's diameter is the height of an adult. Jupiter, the largest planet in the Solar System, is the size of the head, and Earth smaller than the eyeball. The Sun is so huge you could fit a million balls the size of the Earth inside it.

◄----- SHOW ZONE 2 ----►

5

FOLLOW THE **HIGHWAY**

ZONE OVERLOAD FROM SHOW ZONE 1

ZONE

Overload

Let's open up the Sun and take a look inside.

Bypass
BUTTON

LEAP TO **SHOW ZONE 22** TO SEE HOW WE USE THE SUN'S ENERGY ON EARTH.

What's inside the Sun?

The Sun is made up of layers of gas which divide up into different zones.

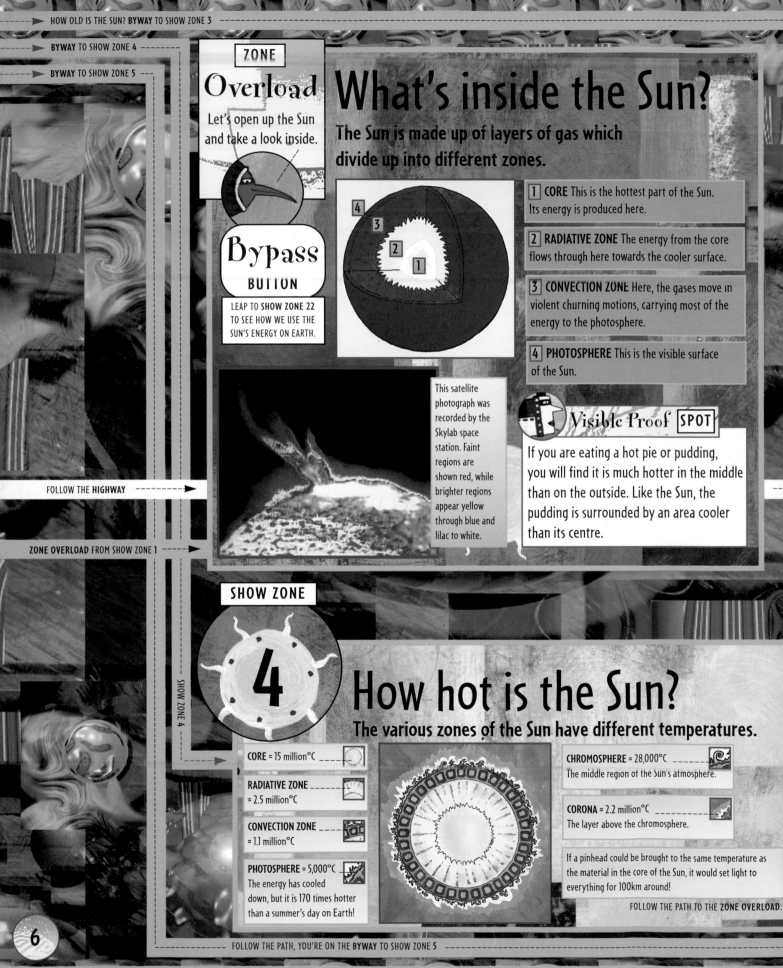

1 CORE This is the hottest part of the Sun. Its energy is produced here.

2 RADIATIVE ZONE The energy from the core flows through here towards the cooler surface.

3 CONVECTION ZONE Here, the gases move in violent churning motions, carrying most of the energy to the photosphere.

4 PHOTOSPHERE This is the visible surface of the Sun.

This satellite photograph was recorded by the Skylab space station. Faint regions are shown red, while brighter regions appear yellow through blue and lilac to white.

Visible Proof **SPOT**

If you are eating a hot pie or pudding, you will find it is much hotter in the middle than on the outside. Like the Sun, the pudding is surrounded by an area cooler than its centre.

SHOW ZONE

SHOW ZONE 4

4

How hot is the Sun?

The various zones of the Sun have different temperatures.

CORE = 15 million°C

RADIATIVE ZONE = 2.5 million°C

CONVECTION ZONE = 1.1 million°C

PHOTOSPHERE = 5,000°C The energy has cooled down, but it is 170 times hotter than a summer's day on Earth!

CHROMOSPHERE = 28,000°C The middle region of the Sun's atmosphere.

CORONA = 2.2 million°C The layer above the chromosphere.

If a pinhead could be brought to the same temperature as the material in the core of the Sun, it would set light to everything for 100km around!

FOLLOW THE PATH TO THE **ZONE OVERLOAD**

FOLLOW THE **HIGHWAY** TO INVESTIGATE A SUNBEAM --->

SHOW ZONE

3

How old is the Sun?

The Sun is about 4,600 million years old! This is ...

10 times as old as the first land plants

2,300 times as old as the human race

39 million times as old as the oldest human being in the world

Bypass

BUTTON

LEAP TO **SHOW ZONE 24** TO LOOK AT THE CHANGING THEORIES OF THE PEOPLE WHO HAVE STUDIED THE SUN.

How do we know this?
Scientists have studied meteorites - pieces of rock that have landed on Earth from space - and pieces of Moon rock which were created at the same time as the Sun. By seeing how much radiation the rocks gave off they were able to find out their age.

FOLLOW THE PATH TO THE **ZONE OVERLOAD**.

ZONE

Overload

Does heat and energy make the Sun shine?

Bypass

BUTTON

WILL THE SUN SHINE FOREVER? TO FIND OUT LEAP TO **SHOW ZONE 5**.

What makes the Sun shine?

A chemical reaction in the Sun's core.

Hydrogen gas changes to helium, creating energy which travels through to the photosphere where it leaves the Sun as heat and light. This causes the Sun to shine.

Sometimes there is a small burst of brightness called a flare, caused by eruptions of gases on the Sun's surface. Flares can produce a jet of flaming gas thousands of kilometres high.

ZONE

Overload

Did the Sun just appear one day?

How was it born?

This is what people think happened...

The Sun is a star. Stars are formed when gases and dust join together and begin to contract under the force of gravity. This produces more and more heat until chemical reactions take place which cause the gases and dust to shine as a star.

5

How does the Sun fit in with the rest of the Universe?

The Sun is one star in the group of 100,000 million stars that form our galaxy. We call our galaxy the Milky Way.

Bypass BUTTON

LEAP TO **SHOW ZONE 21** TO FIND OUT HOW WE USE THE SUN TO RECORD OUR WORLD.

What is the Solar System?

The Sun is at the centre of our Solar System. There are nine planets, including the Earth, that orbit the Sun.

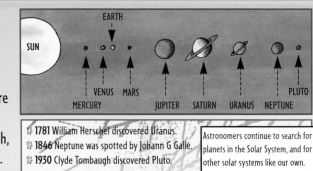

✳ 1781 William Herschel discovered Uranus.
✳ 1846 Neptune was spotted by Johann G Galle.
✳ 1930 Clyde Tombaugh discovered Pluto.

Astronomers continue to search for planets in the Solar System, and for other solar systems like our own.

PLANET	DIAMETER (KM)	DISTANCE FROM SUN (MILLION KM)	TIME TAKEN TO ORBIT THE SUN
MERCURY	4,879	57.9	87.97 EARTH DAYS
VENUS	12,104	108.2	224.7 EARTH DAYS
EARTH	12,756	149.6	365.26 EARTH DAYS
MARS	6,786	227.9	686.98 EARTH DAYS
JUPITER	142,984	778.3	11.86 EARTH YEARS
SATURN	120,536	1,427	29.46 EARTH YEARS
URANUS	51,118	2,870	84.01 EARTH YEARS
NEPTUNE	49,528	4,497	164.8 EARTH YEARS
PLUTO	2,284	5,913	248.5 EARTH YEARS

➤ FOLLOW THE HIGHWAY

➤ WILL THE SUN BE AROUND FOREVER?

6

Does the Sun move?

The Sun spins on its axis and also revolves around the centre of the galaxy.

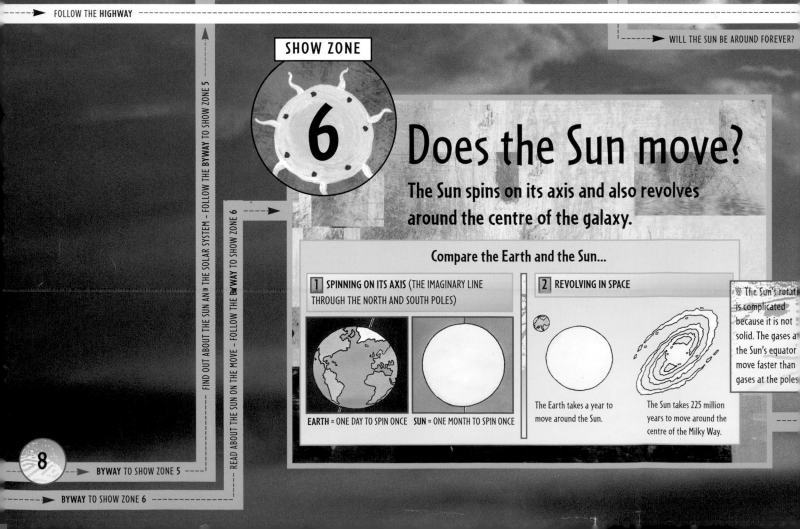

Compare the Earth and the Sun...

1 SPINNING ON ITS AXIS (THE IMAGINARY LINE THROUGH THE NORTH AND SOUTH POLES)

EARTH = ONE DAY TO SPIN ONCE   SUN = ONE MONTH TO SPIN ONCE

2 REVOLVING IN SPACE

The Earth takes a year to move around the Sun.

The Sun takes 225 million years to move around the centre of the Milky Way.

✳ The Sun's rotation is complicated because it is not solid. The gases at the Sun's equator move faster than gases at the poles.

FIND OUT ABOUT THE SUN AND THE SOLAR SYSTEM – FOLLOW THE BYWAY TO SHOW ZONE 5

READ ABOUT THE SUN ON THE MOVE – FOLLOW THE BYWAY TO SHOW ZONE 6

➤ BYWAY TO SHOW ZONE 5

➤ BYWAY TO SHOW ZONE 6

FOLLOW THE PATH TO THE ZONE OVERLOAD

WHEN DOES THE SUN DISAPPEAR FROM THE SKY? FOLLOW THE PATH TO THE ZONE OVERLOAD

ZONE
Overload
Can the Sun really die?

Will the Sun last forever?

Our star will probably die one day. Scientists predict that the Sun will shine for at least another 5,000 million years.

This is what may happen...

1 FAST FORWARD TO 5,000,000,000 YEARS TIME
❉ **TEMPERATURE** The centre of the Sun shrinks and gets hotter. The surface temperature will fall slightly.
❉ **ENERGY** Because of the heat at the centre, the Sun gives off more energy.
❉ **SIZE** The Sun expands by billions of kilometres, stretching out as far as Mercury.

2 The Sun is now a **RED GIANT STAR**. The Sun is too hot for life to exist on Earth.

3 The Sun now shrinks to the size of the Earth and becomes a **WHITE DWARF**.

4 Billions of years later the Sun has used up its energy and lost its heat. It is now a **BLACK DWARF** – a cold, dark globe. Earth is now freezing cold.

How do we know this? Astronomers look at stars that are older than the Sun and watch them go through this process.

This picture shows the corona – the outer layer of the Sun's atmosphere.

Bypass
BUTTON
SEE HOW THE SUN GIVES LIFE TO PLANET EARTH. LEAP TO **SHOW ZONE 13**.

FOLLOW THE **HIGHWAY** TO FIND OUT ABOUT LIGHT

ZONE
Overload
When is the Sun hidden?

What is an eclipse?

The Earth and Moon are constantly moving round the Sun. From Earth, the Sun and Moon appear to be the same size. As a result, when the Moon lies between the Earth and the Sun, it can block out the Sun completely. A shadow is cast on the Earth. We call this an eclipse.

Bypass
BUTTON
LEAP TO **SHOW ZONE 19** TO SEE HOW THE SUN HAS INFLUENCED WHAT PEOPLE BELIEVE.

Visible Proof SPOT

Shine a torch on to an apple. The torch is the Sun and the apple is the Earth. For the Moon, fix a small ball of modelling clay to the end of a metal wire. Place the Moon between the Earth and the Sun and watch as parts of the Earth experience a total eclipse.

Depending on where you are on the Earth, the eclipse may be total or partial. A **TOTAL ECLIPSE** happens if the Moon completely blots out the Sun. When the Moon covers only a part of the Sun, a **PARTIAL ECLIPSE** happens.

SUNLIGHT   SHADOW EARTH

SUN

TOTAL ECLIPSE VIEWED HERE

MOON

During a total eclipse scientists can study the layers of glowing gases.

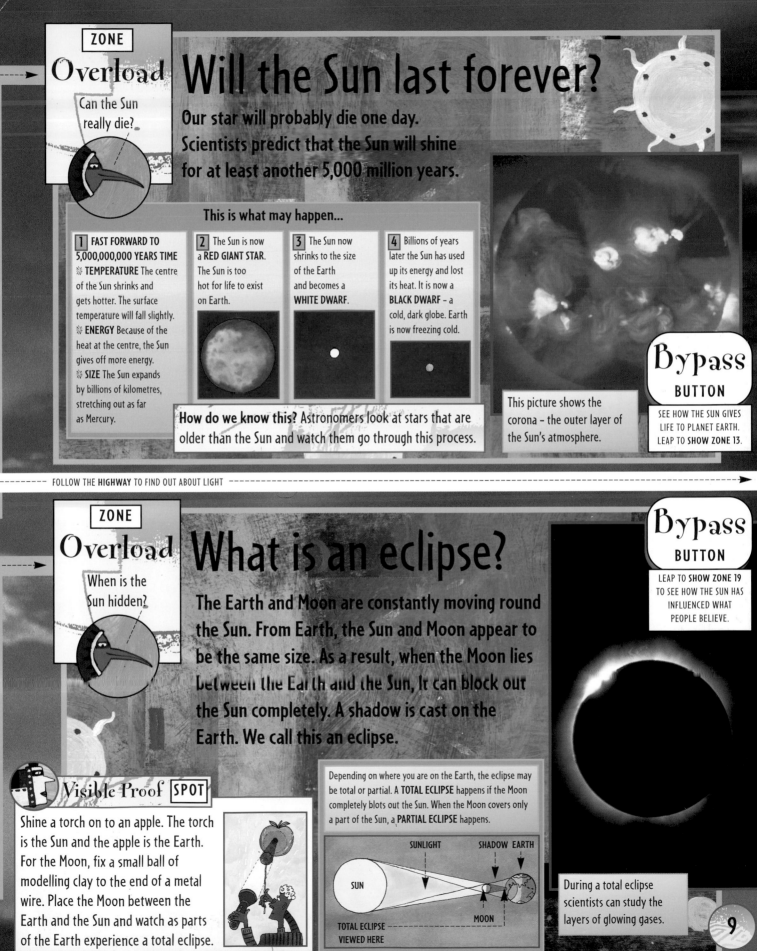

9

Let's take a look at rays of light.

Select
YOUR BYWAY

Sunbeams

7 Who first studied light? (AND WHAT EXACTLY IS IT?)

8 What colour is sunlight? (AND ARE ALL OF THE SUN'S RAYS VISIBLE?)

9 How fast do sunbeams travel?

10 Do all sunbeams reach the Earth?

Whoosh!
What is the speed of light? How can you look back in time?

BYWAY TO SHOW ZONE 7

BYWAY TO SHOW ZONE 8

BYWAY TO SHOW ZONE 9

BYWAY TO SHOW ZONE 10

Who first studied light

People once thought that light was a ray that travelled from th eye to an object, and then back to the eye. Then, in 1665, two men found out more about ligh

Bypass
BUTTON
LEAP TO **SHOW ZONE 11** TO FIND OUT MORE ABOUT LIGHT AND COLOUR.

1 The English scientist **ISAAC NEWTON** discovered that light could be separated into a wide range of colours. He suggested that light was made up of small particles travelling through space.

FOLLOW THE **HIGHWAY** YOU ARE ON THE JOURNEY THAT BRINGS LIFE TO A PLANET

What colour i sunligh

We think of sunligh as being white ligh – but it is actually made up of many different colours.

Visible Proof SPOT

You can see light rays changing direction by carrying out this simple experiment. Put a coloured straw in a glass of water. It seems to bend because light travels more slowly through water.

DO WE KNOW WHAT LIGHT REALLY IS? FOLLOW THE PATH TO THE **ZONE OVERLOAD**.

2 At the same time, the Dutch astronomer **CHRISTIAN HUYGENS** believed that light was made up of waves which travelled at different speeds through different materials – it travelled faster through air than through water. This helped to explain why light could be separated into a spectrum of colours, but not why light travelled in straight lines.

ZONE
Overload
Find out about photons

✳ If an object gives off light it is said to be luminous. The Sun is luminous. Energy is carried from the Sun to the Earth by light.

So what exactly is light?

Light is a form of energy that travels through space.

Today, scientists think that neither Newton nor Huygens were completely right. Light is now thought of as small parcels of energy which we call photons, after the Greek word 'photos' which means 'light'.

LIGHT SOMETIMES BEHAVES LIKE PARTICLES.

LIGHT

LIGHT SOMETIMES BEHAVES LIKE WAVES.

Bypass BUTTON

LEAP TO **SHOW ZONE 12** TO FIND OUT HOW WE FEEL SUNLIGHT.

FOLLOW THE **HIGHWAY** ----➤

LOOKING AT THE SPECTRUM When light passes through a triangular piece of glass called a prism, it separates out into a spectrum of red, orange, yellow, green, blue, indigo and violet. Newton named the seven colours of the spectrum.

WHITE LIGHT ENTERS PRISM

PRISM SEPARATES THE COLOURS BY BENDING THE LIGHT

EACH RAY OF LIGHT IS MADE OF WAVES THAT HAVE DIFFERENT LENGTHS. A WAVELENGTH IS THE DISTANCE FROM THE TOP OF ONE WAVE TO THE TOP OF THE NEXT.

CAN WE SEE ALL OF THE SUN'S RAYS? FOLLOW THE PATH TO THE **ZONE OVERLOAD**.

Visible Proof SPOT

Place a white piece of paper on a table in the sunshine. Carefully tilt a clear piece of plastic towards the paper. See how the sunlight separates out into the colours of the spectrum.

ZONE
Overload
Examine the invisible spectrum

Are all rays visible?

No! The light we see is called 'visible light'. This is a tiny part of the energy that comes from the Sun.

The Sun has an invisible spectrum which includes infra-red and ultra-violet rays that we cannot see. Ultra-violet rays are named because they lie beyond the violet end of the spectrum.

Bypass BUTTON

SEE HOW TOO MUCH ULTRA-VIOLET LIGHT CAN BE HARMFUL. LEAP TO **SHOW ZONE 16**.

9

How fast do sunbeams travel?

Sunbeams travel at the speed of light.

Light travels faster than anything else in the Universe. The speed of light is 299,792km per second.

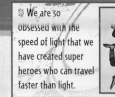

※ We are so obsessed with the speed of light that we have created super heroes who can travel faster than light.

Bypass BUTTON
LEAP TO **SHOW ZONE 22** TO SEE HOW WE CAN USE THE POWER OF SUNLIGHT.

Who first tried to measure the speed of light?

1 In the early 1600s, the Italian scientist **GALILEO GALILEI** tried to measure the speed of light by seeing how long it took to see a light that was being switched on at the top of a distant hill. Unfortunately, light travels too fast for people to measure it on this small scale.

2 In 1675, the Danish astronomer **OLAUS ROEMER** was the first person to prove that light travels at a fixed speed. But the best estimate he could get was 226,000km per second.

3 In 1926, the American physicist **ALBERT MICHELSON** experimented with spinning mirrors to find the speed of light. His measurement was 299,796km per second – only just faster than the real speed.

Visible Proof SPOT

When you look at the stars you are really looking back in time! The light you see actually left the stars many years ago.

FOLLOW THE **HIGHWAY** AND FIND OUT ABOUT THE IMPACT OF THE SUN ON OUR PLANET

BYWAY TO SHOW ZONE 9

FOLLOW THE PATH TO FIND OUT ABOUT THE SPEED OF LIGHT

10

Do all sunbeams reach the Earth?

Bypass BUTTON
LEAP TO **SHOW ZONE 13** TO SEE HOW THE ATMOSPHERE ALLOWS LIFE TO FLOURISH.

Less than half of the sunlight that enters the atmosphere ever reaches the surface of the Earth.

What is the atmosphere? The atmosphere is the layer of gases, water and dust that surrounds the Earth. It is about 700km deep and protects us from the Sun's rays and from pieces of rock, called meteorites, that fall towards the Earth.

BYWAY TO SHOW ZONE 10

ENERGY ENTERING ATMOSPHERE — SUN

3% ABSORBED BY CLOUDS

7% OF SOLAR ENERGY SCATTERED BY ATMOSPHERE

4% REFLECTED BY LAND AND OCEANS

23% REFLECTED BY CLOUDS

SUNBEAM TRAVELS THROUGH ATMOSPHERE

16% ABSORBED BY GASES, WATER VAPOUR AND DUST PARTICLES IN ATMOSPHERE

47% REACHES EARTH AND IS ABSORBED BY EARTH'S SURFACE

THESE ARE AVERAGE FIGURES. WHEN SKIES ARE CLEAR, AROUND 80% OF SUNLIGHT REACHES THE EARTH, AND WHEN IT'S OVERCAST, ONLY 20% MAY HIT THE GROUND.

BYWAY TO SHOW ZONE 9

BYWAY TO SHOW ZONE 10

Phew! I made it through the atmosphere!

Arrival
AT DESTINATION
SUNBEAMS REACH THE
Earth

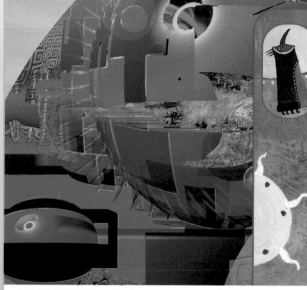

Magic
IN THE ATMOSPHERE

The flares that explode from the surface of the Sun thrust very small atomic particles into space at high speeds. When these particles reach the Earth's atmosphere, they collide with gases, making them glow. From the Earth this looks like an enchanting light show. This effect is called an **AURORA**.

FOLLOW THE **HIGHWAY** AND DISCOVER HOW PEOPLE SEE THE SUNLIGHT AND FEEL IT -------------------->

Auroras are only visible near the poles. These are the Northern lights, or aurora borealis, which can be seen from the Arctic circle. The lights seen from Antarctica are called the aurora australis – or Southern lights.

AEROPLANE
12km above the Earth

SATELLITE
650km above the Earth

Let's go looking for the proof that sunbeams have reached the Earth.

Select

YOUR BYWAY

Sunshine

11 How does sunlight help us to see?
(AND WHEN DO WE SEE SUNLIGHT?)

BYWAY TO SHOW ZONE

12 How do we feel the Sun's heat?

BYWAY TO SHOW ZONE

Observe!
Experiment with shadows and make a rainbow!

FOLLOW THE HIGHWAY

14

11

How does sunlight help us to see?

Objects can only be seen because they reflect the light from something giving out light energy, such as the Sun or a light bulb. The reflected light travels from the object to your eyes. Your eyes send a message to the brain.

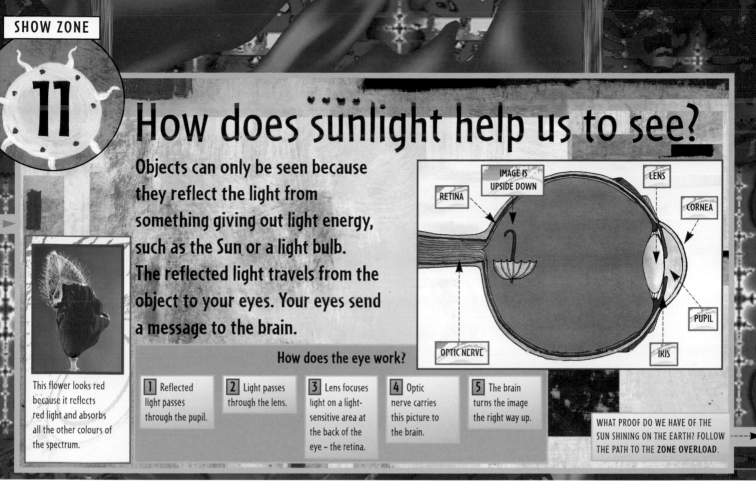

RETINA

IMAGE IS UPSIDE DOWN

LENS

CORNEA

PUPIL

OPTIC NERVE

IRIS

This flower looks red because it reflects red light and absorbs all the other colours of the spectrum.

How does the eye work?

1 Reflected light passes through the pupil.

2 Light passes through the lens.

3 Lens focuses light on a light-sensitive area at the back of the eye – the retina.

4 Optic nerve carries this picture to the brain.

5 The brain turns the image the right way up.

WHAT PROOF DO WE HAVE OF THE SUN SHINING ON THE EARTH? FOLLOW THE PATH TO THE **ZONE OVERLOAD**.

FOLLOW THE **HIGHWAY** TO DISCOVER THE EFFECTS OF THE SUN ON THE PLANET AND ITS PEOPLE

12

How do we feel the Sun's heat?

We feel the warmth of the Sun in two ways: on our skin and in our blood.

How does your brain react to temperature changes?

The brain is the centre of everything you feel and do. It receives signals when your body warms up. You may feel uncomfortable in the heat so your brain sends messages to your muscles, and you move into the shade.

Bypass
BUTTON

LEAP TO **SHOW ZONE 18** TO SEE HOW PEOPLE PROTECT THEMSELVES FROM THE SUN'S RAYS.

What happens when your body sweats?

Your body also reacts to the Sun's heat without you realising it. When you get hot, you may sweat, releasing a cooling salty liquid on to your skin. As your blood warms up, your body slows down its work rate to try to cool down. So your heart may beat slower in hot weather.

Reptiles have a body temperature which changes according to their surroundings. To keep an even temperature, lizards bask in the sunshine at cool times of the day and hide in the shade when the Sun is strong.

ZONE
Overload

Do you need to
see the evidence?

When do we see sunlight?

To understand the effect that sunlight has on the Earth we need to examine night and day, shadows, rainbows and mirages.

1 Night and day

We see sunlight during the day but not at night. This is because the Earth spins on its axis. It goes round once every 24 hours. The side of the Earth that faces the Sun has day and the dark side has night. When the Sun seems to sink in the sky, it is really the Earth turning away from the Sun's light.

Bypass
BUTTON

WITHOUT SUNLIGHT THERE WOULD BE NO LIFE ON EARTH. LEAP TO **SHOW ZONE 13** TO FIND OUT MORE.

Bypass
BUTTON

THE SUN HELPS US TO TELL THE TIME. LEAP TO **SHOW ZONE 20** TO FIND OUT MORE.

ZONE OVERLOAD FROM SHOW ZONE 11

FOLLOW THE HIGHWAY

3 Rainbows

If the Sun starts to shine while it is raining, you may see a rainbow. The rain droplets act like prisms, so when sunlight shines through the drops, the light separates into the colours of the spectrum.

Visible Proof SPOT

Place a mirror at an angle in a plastic dish of water. Stand the dish by a sunny window and wedge a piece of white card between the window ledge and the dish. Watch how the water splits sunlight into the colours of the rainbow.

4 Sunrise and sunset

Although sunlight contains all the colours of the rainbow, at different times of day some of the colours become scattered, and we see those colours that are left behind.

* At **SUNRISE** or **SUNSET**, the light has a longer path through the Earth's atmosphere. More of the blue and green rays are scattered in the atmosphere and the Sun looks red.

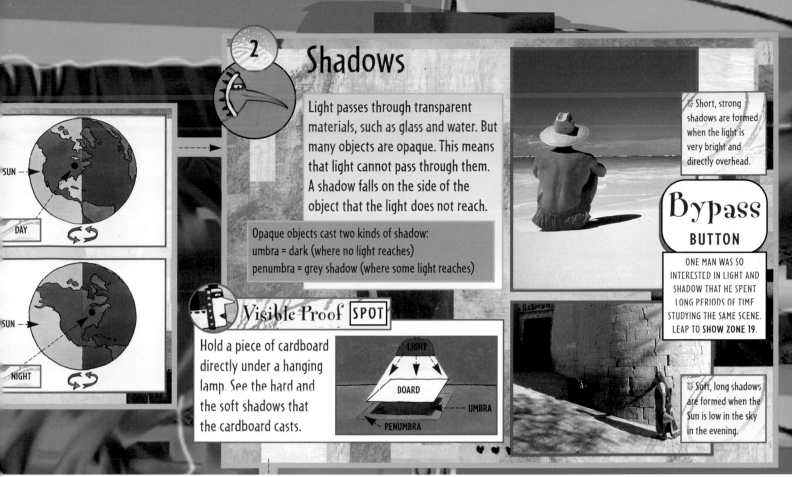

② Shadows

Light passes through transparent materials, such as glass and water. But many objects are opaque. This means that light cannot pass through them. A shadow falls on the side of the object that the light does not reach.

Opaque objects cast two kinds of shadow:
umbra = dark (where no light reaches)
penumbra = grey shadow (where some light reaches)

✳ Short, strong shadows are formed when the light is very bright and directly overhead.

Bypass BUTTON

ONE MAN WAS SO INTERESTED IN LIGHT AND SHADOW THAT HE SPENT LONG PERIODS OF TIME STUDYING THE SAME SCENE. LEAP TO **SHOW ZONE 19.**

✳ Soft, long shadows are formed when the Sun is low in the sky in the evening.

Visible Proof SPOT

Hold a piece of cardboard directly under a hanging lamp. See the hard and the soft shadows that the cardboard casts.

SUN — DAY

SUN — NIGHT

FOLLOW THE **HIGHWAY** AND FIND OUT HOW SUNLIGHT HAS SHAPED OUR PLANET

⑤ Mirages

If you are in a car on a hot day, you may see what seems to be a pool of water on the road ahead. When you reach that spot, the pool will have disappeared. This vanishing image is called a mirage. It happens because light travelling through the hot air just above the ground tends to ripple, producing an image that appears to be water.

✳ At **MIDDAY**, the Sun is high in the sky. Some of the blue light rays are scattered in the Earth's atmosphere. The sky looks blue and the Sun yellow.

GREEN FLASH
The Sun may flash green for an instant just as it sets. This is because the red rays of light are hidden below the horizon and the blue rays are scattered in the atmosphere. This is very rare!

Without the Sun there would be no life on Earth.

Select
YOUR BYWAY

Impact
ON PLANET EARTH

13 How does life depend on the Sun?
(AND WHAT IS PHOTOSYNTHESIS?)

14 Can the Sun change our landscape?
(HOW ARE SPECIES AFFECTED?)

15 How is the weather affected by the Sun?

FOLLOW THE **HIGHWAY**

BYWAY TO SHOW ZONE 13

FOLLOW THE **HIGHWAY**

BYWAY TO SHOW ZONE 13

BYWAY TO SHOW ZONE 14

BYWAY TO SHOW ZONE 15

Weather watch!
The Sun's energy drives the weather. Look out for swirling winds and blazing bush fires!

❋ Today there are more than 10 million different kinds of creature on the Earth!

ZONE
Overloa
All creatures are pa of food chains.

❋ Green plants make their own food. They ar called 'producers'.

How does life depend on the Sun?

Scientists believe that the first forms of life appeared on the Earth more than 3,000 million years ago. The Sun's energy is essential to life.

Living things need the Sun's heat and light to survive. Because the Earth is the right distance from the Sun, life is possible here. Planets nearer the Sun are too hot and those further away are too cold.

Bypass BUTTON

WHAT WILL HAPPEN TO LIFE ON EARTH IF THE ATMOSPHERE IS DAMAGED? LEAP TO **SHOW ZONE 22**.

The greenhouse effect

1 The atmosphere lets sunlight through, which warms the Earth.

2 Some heat reflects off the atmosphere, back towards the Earth.

3 The Earth heats up more.

❋The Earth has a protective layer of air around it called the atmosphere. This stops heat escaping into space, keeping the Earth warm at night when the Sun is not shining. The way the Earth's atmosphere can let light in but not let heat out is called the greenhouse effect.

This satellite picture shows the surface of the planet Venus. It has a very thick atmosphere which keeps much of the Sun's heat in. The surface is too hot for animals and plants to exist.

Visible Proof SPOT

Next time you go into a greenhouse, notice how warm it is. This is because the glass acts like the atmosphere and lets the Sun's heat in but doesn't let all of the heat out.

FOLLOW THE **HIGHWAY** TO DISCOVER HOW THE SUN AFFECTS THE WAY PEOPLE LIVE

HOW DOES THE SUN SUPPLY FOOD FOR LIVING THINGS? FOLLOW THE PATH TO THE **ZONE OVERLOAD**

What is photosynthesis?

This is a process used by green plants to make food by using the Sun's energy.

To make food, plants need to combine carbon dioxide from the air with water from the soil. But they need energy to do this. Chlorophyll, the chemical in plants that makes them green, absorbs light from the Sun. This gives plants the energy to drive the food-making process.

CARBON DIOXIDE IN

OXYGEN OUT

CHLOROPHYLL IN LEAVES ABSORBS LIGHT ENERGY

WATER FROM SOIL IN

Visible Proof SPOT

Take three plates and place a damp piece of blotting paper on each one. Sprinkle some bean seeds on top of the paper. Now put an upturned glass over one set of seeds and a box with a hole in its side over another. Let the third set grow normally. Beansprouts grow faster under the glass, because it is warmer. Those under the box lean towards the light coming through the hole. Soon the plants will need sunlight for healthy growth.

ALL LIVING THINGS ARE PART OF FOOD CHAINS

❋ **PLANTS** (producers) use the Sun to make food by photosynthesis.

❋ **HERBIVORES** (consumers) eat plants.

❋ **CARNIVORES** (consumers) eat herbivores or other carnivores.

THE SUN CHANGES THE LANDSCAPE AND AFFECTS THE SPECIES LIVING ON THE PLANET - **BYWAY** TO SHOW ZONE 14

HOW DOES THE SUN CHANGE THE WEATHER? **BYWAY** TO SHOW ZONE 15

14 Can the Sun change our landscape?

The amount of heat that reaches the ground affects the land we live on.

The Earth has a tilted axis, which means that it sometimes faces the Sun directly (giving us summer) and sometimes at an angle (giving us winter). At the Equator, the Sun's rays strike more directly than anywhere else on the Earth, making it hot. At the poles, the Sun's energy is less direct and is spread over a wide area.

IN HOT REGIONS WITH LITTLE RAIN...
❋ Strong sunshine dries out the ground making huge cracks appear.
❋ Scorching heat can cause bushfires, especially in very dry areas far away from the coast, such as parts of Australia and the USA.

▶ FOLLOW THE **HIGHWAY** --

FOLLOW THE PATH TO DISCOVER THE EFFECT OF THE SUN ON THE LANDSCAPE – BYWAY TO SHOW ZONE 14

15 How is the weather affected by the Sun?

It is the Sun's energy that drives the weather.

The Sun heats water in rivers, lakes and oceans.

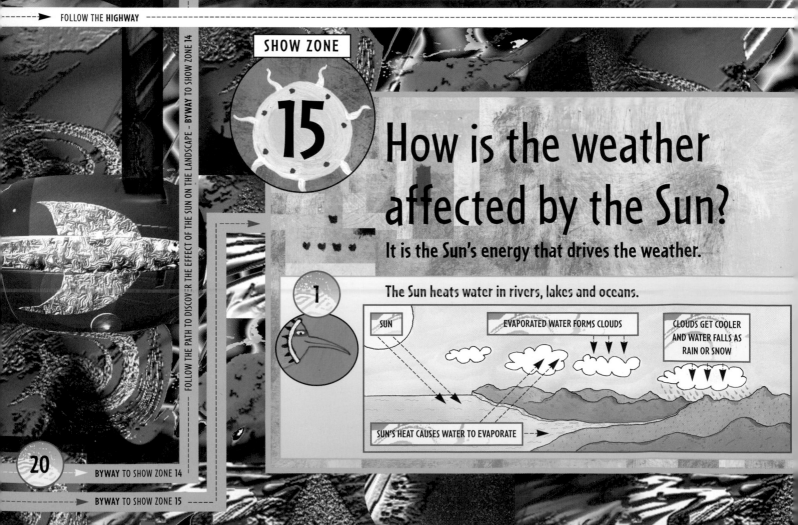

SUN

EVAPORATED WATER FORMS CLOUDS

CLOUDS GET COOLER AND WATER FALLS AS RAIN OR SNOW

SUN'S HEAT CAUSES WATER TO EVAPORATE

BYWAY TO SHOW ZONE 14

BYWAY TO SHOW ZONE 15

IN COLD, ICY REGIONS

❋ Temperatures at the North and South Poles can be as low as -50 °C!

❋ The Sun's heat is not warm enough to melt the ice.

HOW DO ANIMALS AND PLANTS ADAPT TO THESE EXTREME TEMPERATURES? FOLLOW THE PATH TO THE **ZONE OVERLOAD**.

FOLLOW THE PATH TO THE ZONE OVERLOAD

ZONE
Overload

Too hot? Too cold? Protect yourself!

How are species affected?

Plants and animals must adapt to survive warm or cold conditions.

Bypass
BUTTON
HOW DOES THE SUN AFFECT WHERE PEOPLE LIVE? LEAP TO **SHOW ZONE 17**.

STORING WATER

Cactuses, such as the prickly pear, grow in many deserts around the world. They have extremely long roots that grow close to the surface. These roots allow cactuses to collect as much water as possible before it evaporates. They store the water inside their thick fleshy stems.

FINDING COOL PLACES

The gila woodpecker survives in the hot desert by making its nest inside a saguaro cactus where it is much cooler.

COVERING UP

Edelweiss, a plant that grows high up in the mountains, protects itself from the cold by growing woolly hairs on its leaves and flowers.

FOLLOW THE **HIGHWAY** TO DISCOVER WHEN THE SUN CAN BE GOOD AND WHEN IT CAN BE BAD

Visible Proof SPOT

To see how water evaporates, mark the water level of a saucer of water. Leave the saucer for a few hours on a sunny day. The water level will fall, as water evaporates into the atmosphere. In warm weather, the water will evaporate faster.

2 The Sun's heat causes the Earth's swirling winds.

The Sun heats the air surrounding the Earth, causing it to move. Air tends to move from warm to cold areas, so there is a general movement of air from the Equator to the poles.

Bypass
BUTTON
HOW DO WE USE THE ENERGY CREATED BY THE SUN? LEAP TO **SHOW ZONE 22**.

3 The Earth's tilt and movement around the Sun creates the seasons.

The Earth takes one year to move once round the Sun. As the Earth is tilted, parts of it are nearer the Sun at certain times of the year. When it is summer in the northern part of the Earth, it is winter in the southern part of the Earth.

SUMMER

WINTER

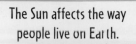

The Sun affects the way people live on Earth.

Select
YOUR BYWAY

Impact
ON THE WAY PEOPLE LIVE

16 Is the Sun good for people?
(AND CAN IT BE BAD?)

17 Does sunlight affect where people live?

18 How do people protect themselves from the Sun?

19 Are people inspired by the Sun?
(AND HAVE THEY EVER WORSHIPPED IT?)

22

BYWAY TO SHOW ZONE 16

FOLLOW THE HIGHWAY

BYWAY TO SHOW ZONE 17

BYWAY TO SHOW ZONE 18

BYWAY TO SHOW ZONE 19

SHOW ZONE

16

Is the Sun good for people?

The right amount of Sun is healthy!

1 BONES The body uses sunlight to produce vitamin D, which is essential to the body because it helps you to absorb calcium, a mineral which strengthens the bones.

2 BREATHING We tend to breathe more deeply and evenly when we sit in the sunshine, and this can help to calm us down.

3 CIRCULATION In hot weather, circulation improves as blood vessels open up. Parts of the body then work more efficiently.

4 HEART People in tropical countries are less likely to have heart attacks than those in colder areas. Scientists believe that one reason this may be is because they receive more sunshine.

SHOW ZONE

17

DAYLIGHT OR DARKNESS
Some towns in Greenland, Canada and Russia are inside the Arctic Circle. In summer months they have 24 hours of sunlight each day. In the winter they have days without any sunlight at all.

Does sunlight affect where people live?

Yes. Far fewer people live in areas where temperatures are extreme.

Some places are simply too hot to live comfortably in and others are too cold. Areas near the North and South Poles get very little sunlight during the winter, while countries near the Equator are hot all year round.

PEOPLE FIND WAYS TO PROTECT THEMSELVES FROM THE SUN'S HEAT - BYWAY TO SHOW ZONE 18

Bypass
BUTTON

HOW DO WE IMITATE THE PHYSICAL NATURE OF THE SUN AND PUT IT TO GOOD USE? FIND OUT IN **SHOW ZONE 23**.

FOLLOW THE PATH TO THE **ZONE OVERLOAD**.

ZONE
Overload

This star has the power to cause damage.

Can the Sun be bad?

Too much Sun can be dangerous.

WHAT IS SUNBURN?
A substance inside our skin called melanin protects us from some of the ultra-violet light in the Sun's rays. Fair skin contains less melanin than darker skin. After a long period of exposure, the Sun's ultra-violet light may cause the skin to burn.

WRINKLES The Sun's drying effect on the skin can create some wrinkles.

SKIN CANCERS Severe sunburn or frequent exposure to sunshine increase the risk of skin cancer, or melanoma.

EYE PROBLEMS Ultra-violet rays in sunlight can cause eye irritation and inflammation.

Visible Proof SPOT

The Sun's rays can also harm buildings and objects. They dry things out and make colours change. Leave a newspaper on a window ledge, where sunlight shines on it. After a few days the pages will be much drier and may have changed colour. Look out for other effects of the Sun such as paint peeling off walls and doors.

---- FOLLOW THE **HIGHWAY** AND DISCOVER HOW PEOPLE USE, AND ARE INSPIRED BY, THE SUN --▸

SHOW ZONE

18

How do people protect themselves?

Take a look at these examples.

SAHARA DESERT, AFRICA
※ World's largest desert.
※ Winter temperature: 10-16°C.
※ Summer temperature: 30-43°C.
※ The same size as the United States but contains 248 million fewer people!

ICE CAP, GREENLAND
※ Greenland is the world's largest island.
※ Winter temperature: around -47°C.
※ Summer temperature: around -11°C.
※ No-one lives permanently on the ice cap. People live in less cold areas on the coast.

Some suntan lotions protect our skin by absorbing the Sun's ultra-violet rays.

In hot countries, buildings may have thick, whitewashed walls to reflect the heat, and small windows to keep out the Sun's rays.

In some hot countries people cover themselves in white clothing. This helps to reflect the heat.

23

Are people inspired by the Sun?

Artists, writers and musicians have been moved by the energy, power and beauty of the Sun.

Bypass
BUTTON
LEAP TO **SHOW ZONE 20** TO SEE HOW SUNLIGHT HELPS US TO KEEP TRACK OF TIME.

BYWAY TO SHOW ZONE 19

✳ **JOSEPH TURNER** (1775-1851), an English artist, made paintings using oil and watercolours which explored the effect of light. He tried to show how bright sunlight coloured the sky and the sea. Some of these paintings were so bright and energetic that people criticised his work for not being realistic enough.

The Fighting Temeraire by Turner.

✳ The Frenchman **CLAUDE MONET** (1840-1926) explored the way light shines outdoors in a series of pictures called 'plein-air' paintings. Monet and his group of painters were named Impressionists after one of Monet's paintings called *Impression - sunrise*. In his *Haystacks* paintings he painted the same view at different times of the day and with changing weather conditions. He showed how objects seem to change with different amounts of sunlight.

✳ **JOSEPH HAYDN** (1732-1809), an Austrian composer wrote a piece of music called *The Creation* which includes a dramatic section which God makes the Sun, bringing light to the Earth.

FOLLOW THE **HIGHWAY** TO FIND OUT HOW PEOPLE USE THE SUN

FOLLOW THE PATH TO FIND OUT ABOUT THE ARTISTS WHO WERE IMPRESSED BY SUNLIGHT

HOW HAVE PEOPLE WORSHIPPED THE SUN? FOLLOW THE PATH TO THE **ZONE OVERLOAD**

ZONE

Overload

People worship the giver of life!

How have people worshipped the Sun?

In ancient times, people thought of the Sun as a god, especially when their survival depended on the heat and light of the Sun to grow their crops.

The mystery of the Sun's eclipse... People thought that the Sun god was angry with them. They prayed and offered sacrifices to calm down their god.

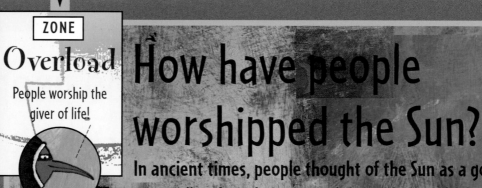

1 The Inca Indians of South America worshipped the Sun, which they called Inti. Inca emperors were believed to have descended from the Sun god and were worshipped as divine beings. The Incas sacrificed llamas and guinea pigs in honour of the Sun, hoping to ensure a good harvest.

2 The Aztecs of Mexico thought of themselves as 'the people of the Sun'. Huitzilopochtli was the god of war and the Sun. This god shared the main temple with Tlaloc, the rain god, who was important to farmers because drought was always a threat.

3 In the old and middle kingdoms of ancient Egypt (2666-1640 BC), people in the Nile Valley worshipped the sun god Re. Egyptians believed that the Sun rising and setting was Re sailing a boat across the sky. They built magnificent temples using pyramid and obelisk shapes – symbols of Re.

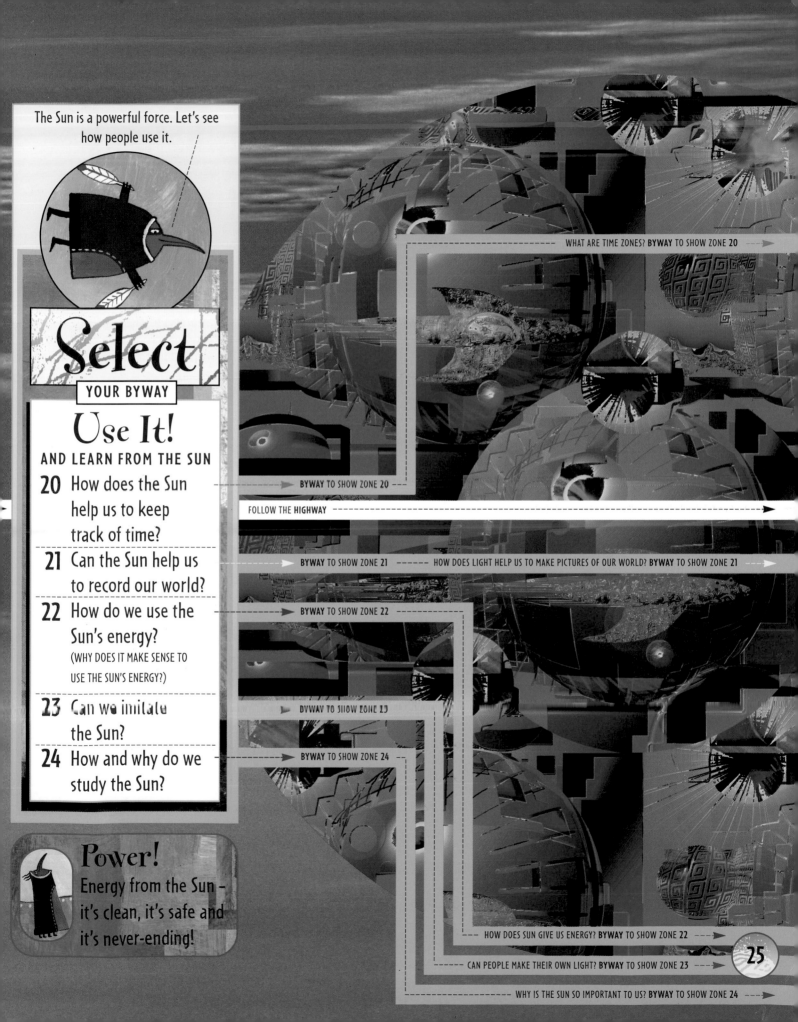

The Sun is a powerful force. Let's see how people use it.

Select
YOUR BYWAY

Use It!
AND LEARN FROM THE SUN

20 How does the Sun help us to keep track of time?

21 Can the Sun help us to record our world?

22 How do we use the Sun's energy?
(WHY DOES IT MAKE SENSE TO USE THE SUN'S ENERGY?)

23 Can we imitate the Sun?

24 How and why do we study the Sun?

Power!
Energy from the Sun – it's clean, it's safe and it's never-ending!

WHAT ARE TIME ZONES? **BYWAY** TO SHOW ZONE **20**

BYWAY TO SHOW ZONE **20**

FOLLOW THE **HIGHWAY**

BYWAY TO SHOW ZONE **21** — HOW DOES LIGHT HELP US TO MAKE PICTURES OF OUR WORLD? **BYWAY** TO SHOW ZONE **21**

BYWAY TO SHOW ZONE **22**

BYWAY TO SHOW ZONE **23**

BYWAY TO SHOW ZONE **24**

HOW DOES SUN GIVE US ENERGY? **BYWAY** TO SHOW ZONE **22**

CAN PEOPLE MAKE THEIR OWN LIGHT? **BYWAY** TO SHOW ZONE **23**

WHY IS THE SUN SO IMPORTANT TO US? **BYWAY** TO SHOW ZONE **24**

20

How does the Sun help us to keep track of time?

We use the Sun to help us measure time.

BYWAY TO SHOW ZONE 20

How did people tell the time before they invented clocks?

Ancient peoples made monuments to the Sun. Some helped them to tell the time. The Incas devised a solar calendar, made up of 12 months according to the Sun's position in the sky.

This giant sundial, made in Jaipur, India, in 1728, was set up to cast shadows on the ground.

How do sundials work?

Sundials show the time according to where the shadow of a pointer falls. The simplest sundial is a stick in the ground. As the position of the Sun changes during the day, the direction of the shadow cast by the pointer also changes.

FOLLOW THE **HIGHWAY**

21

BYWAY TO SHOW ZONE 21

Can the Sun help us to record our world?

※ Daguerrotypes were fragile and captured black and white mirror images of the subjects they were recording.

Yes! People have found ways to control light so that it can be used to make pictures of our world.

Who took one of the first photographs?

The Frenchman **LOUIS DAGUERRE** (1787-1851) was one of the first photographers. In 1839, he invented the daguerrotype. This was a piece of metal with a thin surface of light-sensitive chemicals. When this surface was exposed to the sunlight for a few minutes, an image appeared on the metal.

BYWAY TO SHOW ZONE 22
BYWAY TO SHOW ZONE 23
BYWAY TO SHOW ZONE 24

Visible Proof [SPOT]

See how the Sun moves by making a sundial. Cut out a card circle. Glue or tape a triangular piece of card on to the circle, as shown. Take your sundial outside and mark a shadow at each hour of the day.

The solar year

WE DIVIDE OUR TIME UP INTO...
DAYS
ONE DAY = 24 HOURS
THE TIME THE EARTH TAKES TO ROTATE ONCE
MONTHS
ONE MONTH = BASED ON THE TIME TAKEN
FOR THE MOON TO CIRCLE THE EARTH
YEARS
ONE YEAR = THE TIME IT TAKES FOR THE
EARTH TO CIRCLE THE SUN

The phases of the Moon

The Moon has no light of its own. We can see the Moon because it reflects light from the Sun. So moonlight is really sunlight reflected off the Moon. At different times of the month, the Moon appears to be different shapes. These are called the phases of the Moon and the sequence is repeated every 29 days. Our calendar months, which last between 28 and 31 days, are based on the phases of the Moon.

Stonehenge in England was probably built to track the movement of the Moon and the Sun.

What are time zones?

The world is divided into 24 different time zones. As you move eastwards into each new time zone, you have to set your watch forwards one hour. If you move westwards into each new time zone, you have to set your watch backwards one hour. Some large countries, such as Australia or the USA, contain several different time zones.

WHAT TIME IS IT?

ANCHORAGE
7PM

VANCOUVER
6PM

NEW YORK
3PM

FOLLOW THE **HIGHWAY** AND FIND OUT HOW WE USE THE SUN'S ENERGY

Visible Proof [SPOT]

Gather together some objects, such as a comb, a feather and some paper clips. In a darkened room, take a piece of photographic paper out of its box and arrange the objects on top of it. Shine a lamp over the paper for five minutes. When you remove the objects, you will see where they have left their shapes on the paper. Eventually the paper will be dark all over because the light has reached the whole sheet.

Making a photograph

1. When you take a photograph, the light bouncing off the object travels to the film inside the camera.

2. Photographic film has a coating of a chemical called silver nitrate, which is sensitive to light. After the film has been exposed to light, it is dipped in chemicals so a negative from the light is made.

3. To make a photograph, the negative is placed into a projector. Light shines through the negative onto light-sensitive paper. When this paper is treated with chemicals a photograph is produced.

Bypass BUTTON

PEOPLE CONTINUE TO STUDY SUNLIGHT – WHY? LEAP TO **SHOW ZONE 24**.

HOW DO WE USE THE SUN'S ENERGY? FOLLOW THE PATH TO SHOW ZONE 22

HOW DO WE REPLICATE THE SUN'S LIGHT AND ENERGY? FOLLOW THE PATH TO SHOW ZONE 23

WHAT DO WE HOPE TO LEARN FROM THE SUN? FOLLOW THE PATH TO SHOW ZONE 24

22

How do we use the Sun's energy?

We collect the Sun's energy with solar panels. The weather conditions created by the Sun's energy can also be used to give us power.

How much energy does the Sun provide?
On a sunny day, the energy from the Sun that strikes the ground at any point is the same as that given out by a small electric heater. Each day, the amount of solar energy reaching the Earth is thousands of times greater than the energy we make in power stations.

☀ The Greek inventor, Archimedes, who lived in the 3rd century BC, built a giant solar reflector. He called it a 'Burning Mirror'. He used it to concentrate the Sun's rays on enemy warships, causing them to catch fire.

➤ FOLLOW THE **HIGHWAY**

WHAT IS SO GOOD ABOUT SOLAR POWER? FOLLOW THE PATH TO THE **ZONE OVERLOAD**

ZONE

Overload

Solar energy can save us!

Why does it make sense to use the Sun's energy?

The Sun can supply an energy that will last for millions of years. This energy is also safe and clean.

These fossils were made from the remains of creatures that lived over 500 million years ago.

Fossil fuels, such as coal, gas and oil, are formed from tiny plants and animals. When they died millions of years ago, they were buried in mud. Then, over the years, the mud became hard rock and the rotting plants and animals were turned into fossil fuels. It's important that we learn how to use the Sun's energy because these fossil fuels may soon run out.

➤ **BYWAY** TO SHOW ZONE 22
➤ **BYWAY** TO SHOW ZONE 23
➤ **BYWAY** TO SHOW ZONE 24

What are solar panels?

These are panels that collect the Sun's energy. They are often black, because dark colours absorb more energy than lighter colours. Sometimes these panels are placed on top of houses. Water passes through the panels in pipes and heats up. The warm water then continues to flow around the house, providing hot water for the home. The panels may turn during the day to follow the path of the Sun.

A greenhouse is a simple way of using the Sun's energy. It is used to grow flowers and food and also for drying vegetables so that they can be stored for a long time. The glass lets sunlight in, but does not let much heat escape. This allows the plants to grow.

Can we use the weather?

It is the Sun's energy that sets the Earth's weather in motion. The energy in the wind and rain is stored solar energy because it is not energy which comes directly from the Sun. People can use this energy to create power.

1 WIND POWER

Winds around the world are mainly caused by the Sun heating some parts of the Earth more than others. People build windmills with sails that turn in the wind. These windmills can generate electricity.

2 HYDROELECTRIC POWER

The Sun's heat evaporates water. This makes clouds, and rain falls to make rivers flow. Hydroelectric plants use the flowing rivers to turn wheels and make electricity.

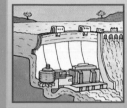

※ Solar energy can be changed into electricity by using panels of solar cells. These cells are made with a material called silicon that gives out electricity when light shines on it.

FOLLOW THE PATH TO THE **ZONE OVERLOAD**.

FOLLOW THE **HIGHWAY** AND MEET THE PEOPLE WHO HAVE STUDIED THE SUN ────────➤

Power that is not safe and clean

When fossil fuels burn, gases are released into the air. Some of these gases, such as sulphur dioxide and nitrogen oxide, dissolve in water droplets in the air and make the water acidic. When rain falls, this acidic water can damage trees, soil and buildings. This is called acid rain.

※ **NUCLEAR POWER** uses the huge amount of energy that is released when the central part of an atom – the nucleus – is split. It causes little pollution – until something goes wrong. In 1986, an explosion at Chernobyl nuclear power station, in the former USSR, released a cloud of radioactive gas into the air. The remains of the power station are pictured below. The Sun is powered by nuclear fusion, where the nuclei of two or more atoms are joined together. If scientists can achieve nuclear fusion on Earth, it would give us a limitless supply of clean, safe power.

Visible Proof SPOT

You can use vinegar, a weak acid, to see how acid rain destroys plants. Dip some leaves in a saucer of vinegar. Then leave them with their stalks resting in the vinegar for a few days. Soon the leaves turn brown and die as the acid starts to eat away at them – from both the inside and the outside.

TO FIND OUT ABOUT MAKING ARTIFICIAL LIGHT – FOLLOW THE **BYWAY** TO SHOW ZONE 23 ────➤

TO FIND OUT HOW WE USE TELESCOPES TO STUDY THE SUN – FOLLOW THE **BYWAY** TO SHOW ZONE 24 ────➤

23

Can we imitate the Sun?

Natural light comes from the Sun and cannot be controlled. Artificial light, however, comes from sources that we can control.

Seeing in the dark

People have found ways of imitating the effect of the Sun, making light so that they can see even when there is no sunlight. At first, people used fire and candles, then they discovered oil and gas and used them to power lamps. Today, electric lights are used throughout the world.

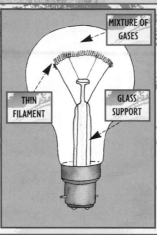

MIXTURE OF GASES

THIN FILAMENT

GLASS SUPPORT

How does an electric light work?

1. Electricity is switched on, with a light switch.
2. Electricity flows through a thin coil of tungsten metal called a filament.
3. The filament heats up to around 2,700°C.
4. It glows white and gives out light.
5. The filament is surrounded by gases other than air. If air could reach the filament it would burn up.

Neon lights are often used for street signs. They do not have a filament. Instead, they are tubes filled with a gas called neon that produces light when electricity passes through it.

FOLLOW THE **HIGHWAY** TO THE END OF YOUR JOURNEY – A DISTANCE OF **150 MILLION KILOMETRES**

24

How and why do we study the Sun?

We examine the movement and physical nature of the Sun because we know that it is crucial for our survival on Earth. The more we know about the 'bringer of life' the more we can learn about our world, and stars other than the Sun.

SUN STUDY TELLS US ABOUT OUR SOLAR SYSTEM AND OTHER STARS.	
DATE	**THE ASTRONOMER**
AD 127–41	**PTOLEMY OF ALEXANDRIA**, an astronomer, announced that the Earth was stationary at the centre of the Universe. He thought that the Sun, Moon and the planets all circled the Earth.
1543	**NICOLAUS COPERNICUS**, a Polish astronomer, stated that the Earth and other planets circled around the Sun.
1904	**GEORGE ELLERY HALE**, an American astronomer, set up the Mount Wilson Observatory in California, USA, in 1904. This included instruments for studying the Sun. Hale realised that by understanding the Sun, you could find out about other stars.

※ **CORONAGRAPHS** photograph the Sun's corona, the gases surrounding the Sun, by blocking out the light from the photosphere and chromosphere. This is like creating an artificial eclipse.

BYWAY TO SHOW ZONE 23

BYWAY TO SHOW ZONE 24

Ultra-violet rays

Ultra-violet light is the light that makes your skin tan or burn. Overexposure to it can cause skin cancer. The Sun is the major source of ultra-violet light but it can be produced artificially by passing electricity through particular gases.

1 Sun lamps give out ultra-violet light and are used for tanning. People need to take care because the rays are much stronger than those of sunlight.

2 Ultra-violet rays can also be used to kill bacteria and viruses. Hospitals use them to sterilise the air and equipment in operating rooms.

※ **LASERS** are instruments that can produce narrow, powerful beams of light. Lasers are precise, safe and sterile so they are ideal tools for surgery, particularly eye surgery.

How do astronomers study sunlight today?

Astronomers use powerful telescopes to take detailed photographs of sunspots and storms on the Sun's surface. The Kitt Peak National Observatory in Arizona, USA, has one of the world's largest telescopes. It is positioned on a mountain about 2,000m high. Being above the clouds, there is less water vapour to look through. The turbulence in the Earth's atmosphere sometimes makes it difficult to see a clear image of the Sun's surface.

HOW DOES IT WORK?

At the top of a tower there is a flat mirror, 2.1m wide. It turns and follows the Sun. This mirror bounces the sunlight down a tunnel 150m long to a curved mirror, which reflects the sunlight on to another mirror. This mirror projects it into a viewing room. The final image is nearly 1m wide.

SKYLAB, the first space station, was launched in 1973. Telescopes on board measured different types of radiation from the Sun.

From the source –

Sun

to the destination –

Earth

A journey that happens everyday, bringing heat, light and energy to a planet that would otherwise be a barren rock spiralling in the Universe.

Imagine!

Is the Sun the only star giving life to a planet, or is there life elsewhere in another galaxy?

Index

acid rain 29
aeroplanes 13
animals 19, 21
Archimedes 28
artists 24
astronomers 8, 9, 11, 30, 31
atmosphere 5, 12, 13, 16, 17, 19, 21, 31
atoms 13, 29
auroras 13
axis 8, 16, 20
Aztecs 24

bacteria 31
black dwarves 9
blood 15, 22
bones 22
brain 15
breathing 22
bushfires 20

cactuses 21
calendars 26
cameras 27
cancer 23, 31
candles 30
carbon dioxide 19
carnivores 19
Chernobyl 29
chlorophyll 19
chromosphere 6, 30
clouds 12, 20
coal 28
cold 9, 19, 20, 21, 22, 23
colours 5, 10, 11, 15, 16, 29

consumers 19
convection zone 6
Copernicus, Nicolaus 30
core 6, 7
cornea 15
corona 6, 9, 30
coronagraphs 30

Daguerre, Louis 26
daguerrotype 26
day 8, 16, 22
deserts 21, 23
dust 7, 12

Earth 5, 7, 8, 9, 12, 13, 16, 17, 18, 19, 20, 21, 30, 31
eclipses 9, 24, 30
Egyptians 24
electricity 28, 29, 30, 31
electric lights 30
energy 6, 7, 9, 11, 12, 19, 20, 24, 28, 29
Equator 8, 20, 21, 22
evaporation 20, 21
eyes 15

filaments 30
flares 7, 13
food chains 18, 19
fossil fuels 28, 29
fuels 5, 28, 29

galaxies 8
Galilei, Galileo 12
Galle, Johann 8

gases 4, 5, 6, 7, 8, 9, 12, 13, 28, 29, 30, 31
granules 4
gravity 7
greenhouse effect 19
greenhouses 19, 29
Hale, George 30
Haydn, Joseph 24
heart 22
heat 6, 7, 9, 15, 17, 19, 20, 21, 22, 23
helium 5, 7
herbivores 19
Herschel, William 8
Huitzilopochtli 24
Huygens, Christian 11
hydroelectric power 29
hydrogen 5, 7

Impressionists 24
Incas 24, 26
infra-red light 11, 31
Inti 24
iris 15

Jupiter 5, 8

landscapes 20
lasers 31
lens 15
life 18, 19
light 5, 7, 9, 10, 11, 12, 13, 15, 16, 17, 19, 21, 22, 23, 24, 26, 27, 29, 30, 31
light bulbs 15, 30

Mars 8
melanin 23
melanoma 23
Mercury 8, 9
meteorites 7, 12
Michelson, Albert 12
Milky Way 8
mirages 17
Monet, Claude 24
month 27
Moon 7, 9, 27
musicians 24

negative images 27
neon lights 30
Neptune 8
Newton, Isaac 10
night 16, 22
nuclear fusion 29
nuclear power 29

oceans 12, 20
oil 28, 30
optic nerve 15
orbits 8, 21

penumbra 17
photographs 26, 27, 30
photons 11
photosphere 4, 6, 7, 30
photosynthesis 19
plants 18, 19, 21, 29
Pluto 8
poles 8, 20, 21, 22
pollution 28, 29

prisms 11, 16
producers 18
Ptolemy 30
pupil 15

radiation 7, 29
radiative zone 6
rain 16, 20, 29
rainbows 16
Re 24
reptiles 15
retina 15
Roemer, Olaus 11

satellites 6, 13, 19
Saturn 8
seeds 19
shadows 9, 17, 26, 27
silicon 29
size 5, 8, 9
skin 15
Skylab 31
solar cells 28, 29
solar panels 28, 29
solar system 5, 8
spectrum 5, 11, 15, 16
stars 5, 7, 9, 12, 30
Stonehenge 27
summer 21, 22, 23
sunburn 23
sundials 26, 27
sun lamps 31
sunrises 16, 24
sunsets 16, 24
suntan lotions 23

supergiants 5
sweating 15

tanning 23, 31
telescopes 31
time 8, 12, 22, 24, 26, 27
time zones 27
Tombaugh, Clyde 8
transparent objects 17
Turner, Joseph 24

ultra-violet light 11, 23, 31
umbra 17
Universe 8, 12, 30
Uranus 8

Venus 8, 19
viruses 31

water 11, 12, 17, 20, 21, 29
wavelengths 11
waves 10, 11
weather 20, 24, 29
white dwarves 9
wind power 29
winds 21, 29
winter 21, 22, 23
worship 24
wrinkles 23

year 8, 21, 27
yellow dwarves 5

zones 6

※ PICTURE CREDITS Front cover: left, right: Science Photo Library; centre: Pictor. Back cover: Science Photo Library. Inside: P1 background: Pictor. P3 top: Science Photo Library; bottom: Werner Forman Archive/Egyptian Museum, Cairo. P5 NASA/Science Photo Library. P6 NASA/Science Photo Library. P7 top, bottom: NASA/Science Photo Library. P8 background: Pictor; top: Science Photo Library. P9 background: Pictor; top, bottom: Science Photo Library. P10 top left, bottom: Pictor; top right: Science Museum/Science & Society. P11 Science Photo Library. P12 background: Pictor. P13 background: Pictor; left, right: Science Photo Library. P15 top: Science Photo Library; bottom left: Tony Stone; bottom right: Pictor. P16 left: Science Photo Library; right: Pictor. P17 top right, centre right: Tony Stone; bottom right: Science Photo Library; bottom left: Pictor. P18 bottom: Pictor; top: Tony Stone. P19 top: NASA/Science Photo Library. p20 Science Photo Library. P21 top left, centre right: Pictor; top centre left: Planet Earth Pictures; top centre right, top right: Oxford Scientific Films; bottom left, bottom right: Science Photo Library. P22 Tony Stone. P23 top left, bottom left: Tony Stone; top centre: Science Photo Library; top right, bottom centre, bottom right: Pictor. P24 background: Pictor; top: Bridgeman Art Library/National Gallery London; bottom right: Bridgeman Art Library/British Museum; bottom left: Mary Evans; P25 background: Pictor. P26 bottom: Werner Forman Archive; p27 top right: Science Photo Library; top left: Pictor. P28 top, bottom: Science Photo Library. P29 top left: Pictor; top right: Eye Ubiquitous; bottom left, bottom right: Science Photo Library. P30 Pictor. P31 top left, top right: Science Photo Library; bottom right: Pictor.